YO-BYV-551

THE VANCOUVER SUN

the best

desserts

BY CANADA'S BEST-SELLING AUTHORS FROM *THE VANCOUVER SUN* TEST KITCHEN

RUTH PHELAN AND BRENDA THOMPSON

Published by Pacific Newspaper Group,
A division of CanWest MediaWorks Publications Inc.
1-200 Granville Street
Vancouver, B.C.
V6C 3N3

Pacific Newspaper Group President and Publisher:
        Dennis Skulsky

Library and Archives Canada Cataloguing in Publication

Phelan, Ruth, 1960-
        The best desserts / Ruth Phelan, Brenda Thompson.

(The best)
Includes index.
Co-published by: Pacific Newspaper Group.
ISBN 1-897229-02-X

        1. Desserts. I. Thompson, Brenda, 1944- II. Title. III. Series: The
best (Toronto, Ont.)

TX773.P468 2005   641.8'6   C2005-904859-X

All photographs by Peter Battistoni

Home Economists: Ruth Phelan & Brenda Thompson

Nutritional Analysis: Jean Fremont

Edited by Shelley Fralic

Printed and bound in Canada by Friesens

First Edition

10 9 8 7 6 5 4 3 2 1

Introduction

From elegant rich tarts to simple moist cakes reminiscent of grandma's kitchen, there is a recipe for every occasion in this collection of the best dessert recipes to come out of *The Vancouver Sun* Test Kitchen.

Our delectable treats include favourite ingredients like fresh seasonal fruits, luscious chocolate and tangy lemons along with some new taste twists, from fresh lavender and seductively aromatic vanilla beans to flavourful liqueurs. This five-star collection has been divided into three categories — from the oven, fridge and freezer — and is illustrated with mouth-watering photographs taken by Sun photographer Peter Battistoni.

Whether you're looking for a grand finale to that special dinner, or just something sweet to go with afternoon coffee, your friends and family will love these unforgettable desserts.

We hope you enjoy this third collection in our *The Best* cookbook series.

Ruth Phelan
Brenda Thompson
Vancouver, B.C.
October, 2005

A Cook's Guide to the Recipes

- Use medium-size fresh fruit and vegetables unless specified otherwise.

- To melt chocolate, put chocolate in heatproof bowl set over saucepan of hot, not simmering water until chocolate is about three-quarters melted (the water should not touch the bottom of the bowl), stirring occasionally. Remove bowl from saucepan and continue stirring until chocolate is melted and smooth.

- Avoid the possibility of buying rancid nuts and purchase from a store that has a high turnover. Don't use any nuts that have even a hint of rancidity — no technique or cooking method will mask their bitter, nasty flavour.

- To toast nuts, spread nuts on rimmed baking sheet. Bake at 350 F (180 C) until fragrant and lightly browned — sliced or slivered almonds take about 5 minutes and pecan halves take 6 to 8 minutes. Let cool.

- To toast hazelnuts, spread nuts on rimmed baking sheet. Bake at 350 F (180 C) for 8 to 10 minutes or until fragrant and lightly browned. Transfer nuts to clean tea towel; roll nuts around, inside towel, to remove as much of the skins as possible. Let cool.

- Beating or stirring. When the recipe instructions specify "beat" ingredients, this should be done with an electric mixer. "Stirring" is done by hand with a wooden or metal spoon.

- Measuring dry ingredients. Use dry measuring cups, which come in imperial sets of ¼, ½, ⅓ and 1 cup, and metric sets of 50, 75, 125 and 250 mL. Be sure to measure dry ingredients, such as flour and cocoa, correctly; stir and lightly spoon into a dry measuring cup until filled slightly above the rim, then level off with the straight edge of a knife. (Do not shake or tap cup, this will increase the amount of flour in the cup and result in a dough or batter that is too stiff.)

- Checking for doneness. Because oven temperatures and burners vary slightly always check for doneness a few minutes before the specified time. A few minutes can make the difference between a baked and overbaked cake or pastry, or a cooked and overcooked filling.

- Butter is salted.

- Milk is 2 per cent M.F.

Apple Ginger Galette (recipe on following page)

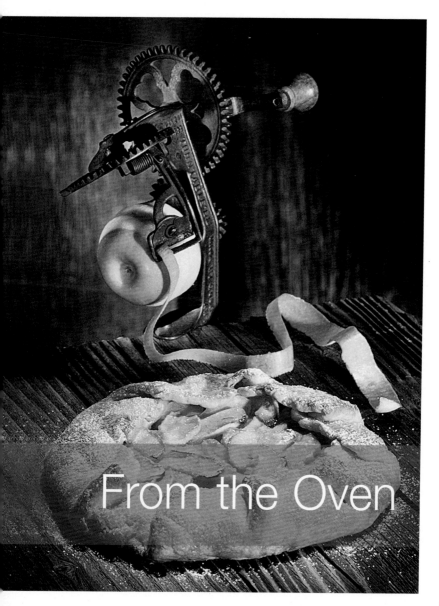

From the Oven

Apple Ginger Galette

Pastry

2	cups (500 mL) all-purpose flour
1	tablespoon (15 mL) granulated sugar
½	teaspoon (2 mL) salt
⅓	cup (75 mL) cold butter, cubed
⅓	cup (75 mL) cold shortening, cubed
6	tablespoons (90 mL) ice water, about
1	large egg yolk
1	teaspoon (5 mL) white vinegar

Filling

⅓	cup (75 mL) granulated sugar
2	tablespoons (30 mL) all-purpose flour
6	cups (1.5 L) thinly sliced, peeled apples
1	tablespoon (15 mL) fresh lemon juice
1	tablespoon (15 mL) finely chopped crystallized ginger
1	teaspoon (5 mL) finely grated lemon zest

Other ingredients

	Milk
2	teaspoons (10 mL) granulated sugar
	Icing sugar

Pastry: In large bowl, combine flour, sugar and salt. Using pastry blender or two knives, cut in butter and shortening until mixture resembles coarse crumbs with a few larger pieces.

In small bowl, whisk together water, egg yolk and vinegar. With fork, quickly stir egg yolk mixture into flour mixture, 1 tablespoon (15 mL) at a time, until dough holds together. Using your hands, bring dough together and shape into a disc. Wrap in plastic wrap and refrigerate for 30 minutes. *(Make ahead: Dough can be refrigerated for up to 1 day.)*

On floured surface, roll out dough into 14-inch (36 cm) circle, leaving edges rough. Carefully roll dough around rolling pin and transfer it to centre of large rimless baking sheet.

Filling: In small bowl, combine sugar and flour. In large bowl, toss apples with lemon juice; add flour mixture and toss to coat. Add ginger and zest; toss.

Pile apple mixture in centre of dough, leaving a 2½-inch (6 cm) border. Fold dough overhang up over filling to form attractive ragged edge; brush top of dough with milk and sprinkle with 2 teaspoons (10 mL) granulated sugar.

Bake at 425 F (220 C) for 15 minutes. Reduce heat to 375 F (190 C) and bake an additional 35 to 40 minutes or until apples are tender and filling is bubbly, covering loosely with foil during last 15 minutes of baking time. Let cool on baking sheet on rack for 10 minutes, then transfer galette to rack and let cool completely. Just before serving, dust galette with icing sugar.

Tips

• *Chilling the dough for at least 30 minutes will make it more manageable and easier to roll.*

• *We used Granny Smith apples to make this rustic free-form pie known as a galette, but any baking apple will do.*

• *For superior flavour and texture, buy Australian chunky crystallized ginger. It's darker in colour and has a more peppery taste than the thinner, paler slices of crystallized ginger that are heavily coated with coarse sugar.*

Makes 8 servings. PER SERVING: 394 cal, 4 g pro, 17 g fat, 59 g carb.

Rhubarb Cherry Galette

Pastry

2	cups (500 mL) all-purpose flour
1	tablespoon (15 mL) granulated sugar
½	teaspoon (2 mL) salt
⅓	cup (75 mL) cold butter, cubed
⅓	cup (75 mL) cold shortening, cubed
6	tablespoons (90 mL) ice water, about
1	large egg yolk
1	teaspoon (5 mL) white vinegar

Filling

1¼	cups (300 mL) granulated sugar
¼	cup (50 mL) all-purpose flour
6	cups (1.5 L) sliced (½-inch/1 cm thick) rhubarb
⅓	cup (75 mL) dried sweet cherries, chopped coarse
2	teaspoons (10 mL) finely grated orange zest
1	teaspoon (5 mL) pure vanilla extract

Other ingredients

	Milk
2	teaspoons (10 mL) granulated sugar
	Icing sugar

Pastry: In large bowl, combine flour, sugar and salt. Using pastry blender or two knives, cut in butter and shortening until mixture resembles coarse crumbs with a few larger pieces.

In small bowl, whisk together water, egg yolk and vinegar. With fork, quickly stir egg yolk mixture into flour mixture, 1 tablespoon (15 mL) at a time, until dough holds together. Using your hands, bring dough together and shape into a disc. Wrap in plastic wrap and refrigerate for 30 minutes. *(Make ahead: Dough can be refrigerated for up to 1 day.)*

On floured surface, roll out dough into 14-inch (36 cm) circle, leaving edges rough. Carefully roll dough around rolling pin and transfer it to centre of large rimless baking sheet.

Filling: In small bowl, combine sugar and flour. In large bowl, toss rhubarb with flour mixture to coat. Add cherries and zest; toss. Drizzle with vanilla and toss to mix.

Pile rhubarb mixture in centre of dough, leaving a 2½-inch (6 cm) border. Fold dough overhang up over filling to form attractive ragged edge; brush top of dough with milk and sprinkle with 2 teaspoons (10 mL) granulated sugar.

Bake at 425 F (220 C) for 15 minutes. Reduce heat to 375 F (190 C) and bake an additional 35 to 40 minutes or until rhubarb is tender and filling is bubbly, covering loosely with foil during the last 15 minutes of baking time. Let cool on baking sheet on rack for 10 minutes, then transfer galette to rack and let cool completely. Just before serving, dust galette with icing sugar.

Tip: *You'll need about 1¾ pounds (850 g) rhubarb to yield about 6 cups (1.5 L) sliced.*

Makes 8 servings. PER SERVING: 441 cal, 5 g pro, 17 g fat, 70 g carb.

Blueberry Cobbler

Filling

5	cups (1.25 L) blueberries
2	tablespoons (30 mL) fresh lemon juice
⅔	cup (150 mL) granulated sugar
3	tablespoons (45 mL) all-purpose flour
½	teaspoon (2 mL) ground cinnamon
2	tablespoons (30 mL) butter, at room temperature

Topping

1	cup (250 mL) all-purpose flour
2	tablespoons (30 mL) granulated sugar
1½	teaspoons (7 mL) baking powder
¼	teaspoon (1 mL) salt
⅓	cup (75 mL) butter, at room temperature
3	tablespoons (45 mL) milk
1	large egg, lightly beaten

Filling: Put blueberries in large bowl; sprinkle with lemon juice. In small bowl, combine sugar, flour and cinnamon; sprinkle evenly over blueberries and stir to mix. Spread blueberry mixture evenly in ungreased 8-inch (20 cm) square baking dish. Dot with butter.

Topping: In medium bowl, combine flour, sugar, baking powder and salt. Using back of fork, cut in butter until mixture resembles fine crumbs. In small bowl, whisk together milk and egg. Add to flour mixture; using fork, stir to mix. Drop dough by 9 equal spoonfuls onto blueberry mixture.

Bake at 375 F (190 C) for 40 minutes or until topping is golden brown and juices are bubbling in the centre, covering loosely with foil during last 10 minutes of baking time. Serve warm with ice cream, if desired.

Tip: Substitute 3 cups (750 mL) sliced peeled peaches for 3 cups (750 mL) of the blueberries.

Makes 9 servings. PER SERVING: 267 cal, 3 g pro, 10 g fat, 43 g carb.

Blueberry Buckle

Topping

¼	cup (50 mL) all-purpose flour
¼	cup (50 mL) packed brown sugar
¼	cup (50 mL) granulated sugar
½	teaspoon (2 mL) ground cinnamon
¼	cup (50 mL) butter, at room temperature

Batter

¾	cup (175 mL) granulated sugar
¼	cup (50 mL) butter, at room temperature
2	large eggs
1	teaspoon (5 mL) grated orange zest
1	teaspoon (5 mL) pure vanilla extract
2	cups (500 mL) all-purpose flour
2	teaspoons (10 mL) baking powder
½	teaspoon (2 mL) salt
½	cup (125 mL) buttermilk
2	cups (500 mL) blueberries

Topping: In small bowl, combine flour, brown and granulated sugars, and cinnamon. Using back of fork, cut in butter until mixture is crumbly.

Batter: In large bowl, beat sugar and butter until fluffy. Beat in eggs, one at a time. Beat in zest and vanilla.

In medium bowl, combine flour, baking powder and salt. Stir flour mixture and buttermilk alternately into egg mixture, beginning and ending with flour mixture. Stir in blueberries. Spread batter evenly in greased 8-inch (20 cm) square baking dish. Sprinkle evenly with topping.

Bake at 375 F (190 C) for 40 to 45 minutes or until top springs back when lightly pressed in the centre, covering loosely with foil during last 15 minutes of baking time. Let cool in baking dish on rack. Cut into squares.

Tip: Don't overmix batter; stir just until dry ingredients are moistened.

Makes 9 servings. PER SERVING: 335 cal, 6 g pro, 10 g fat, 56 g carb.

Rhubarb Ginger Crisp

Topping

1	cup (250 mL) quick-cooking oats (not instant)
⅓	cup (75 mL) all-purpose flour
½	cup (125 mL) packed brown sugar
½	teaspoon (2 mL) salt
½	teaspoon (2 mL) ground cinnamon
⅓	cup (75 mL) butter, melted

Filling

6	cups (1.5 L) sliced (½-inch/1 cm thick) rhubarb
2	teaspoons (10 mL) finely grated orange zest
1	tablespoon (15 mL) fresh orange juice
1	tablespoon (15 mL) finely chopped, drained preserved ginger
1	tablespoon (15 mL) syrup from preserved ginger
1¼	cups (300 mL) granulated sugar
2	tablespoons (30 mL) all-purpose flour
1	large egg, beaten

Topping: In medium bowl, combine oats, flour, sugar, salt and cinnamon. Using fork, stir in butter until mixture is crumbly.

Filling: In large bowl, combine rhubarb, orange zest and juice, and preserved ginger and syrup; mix well. In small bowl, combine sugar and flour. Stir in egg (mixture will be thick); add to rhubarb mixture and mix well. Spread rhubarb mixture evenly in ungreased 8-inch (20 cm) square baking dish. Sprinkle evenly with topping.

Bake at 350 F (180 C) for 60 minutes or until rhubarb is tender, covering with foil if browning too quickly.

Winter Crisp Variation: Omit rhubarb filling and substitute a frozen fruit filling. Put 1 (600 g) package (about 5 cups/1.25 L) of frozen mixed unsweetened fruit (blueberries, peaches and strawberries) in large bowl. (Cut any extra large wedges of frozen peach in half crosswise.) Add ⅓ cup (75 mL) granulated sugar and toss.

In small bowl, combine 1 tablespoon (15 mL) fresh lemon juice and ½ teaspoon (2 mL) pure vanilla extract; sprinkle over fruit mixture and toss. Transfer fruit mixture to ungreased 8-inch (20 cm) square baking dish and spread evenly. Sprinkle evenly with topping. Cover tightly with foil and bake at 375 F (190 C) for 35 minutes. Uncover and bake for about 30 minutes or until bubbly and fruit is tender.

Tip: *Ginger lovers can increase the chopped preserved ginger in the rhubarb filling to 2 tablespoons (30 mL).*

Makes 6 servings. PER SERVING: 472 cal, 5 g pro, 12 g fat, 90 g carb.

Apple Pear Cranberry Crisp

Topping

1	cup (250 mL) quick-cooking oats (not instant)
⅔	cup (150 mL) packed brown sugar
½	cup (125 mL) all-purpose flour
¼	teaspoon (1 mL) ground cardamom
½	cup (125 mL) butter, melted
½	cup (125 mL) blanched almonds, chopped coarse

Filling

5	pears, peeled, cored and cut into 1-inch (2.5 cm) pieces
3	large apples, peeled, cored and cut into 1-inch (2.5 cm) pieces
2	cups (500 mL) cranberries
½	cup (125 mL) granulated sugar
2	tablespoons (30 mL) chopped, drained preserved ginger
	Grated zest of 1 orange

Topping: In medium bowl, combine oats, sugar, flour and cardamom. Using fork, stir in butter until mixture is crumbly. Stir in almonds.

Filling: In large bowl, combine pears, apples, cranberries, sugar, ginger and zest. Spread fruit mixture evenly in ungreased 13x9-inch (33x23 cm) baking dish. Sprinkle evenly with topping.

Bake at 350 F (180 C) for 50 to 55 minutes or until apples are tender.

Tips

• *We used Golden Delicious apples but you could substitute your favourite baking apple.*
• *Preserved ginger is similar to crystallized ginger but instead of being coated with sugar, the translucent pieces of ginger are packed in a jar with syrup. Both the ginger and syrup can be used to flavour sweet and savoury dishes.*

Makes 8 servings. PER SERVING: 479 cal, 5 g pro, 19 g fat, 78 g carb.

Blackberry Mango Crisp

Topping

1½   cups (375 mL) quick-cooking oats (not instant)
1   cup (250 mL) packed brown sugar
½   cup (125 mL) all-purpose flour
¾   teaspoon (4 mL) salt
½   teaspoon (2 mL) ground cinnamon
½   cup (125 mL) butter, at room temperature

Filling

3   cups (750 mL) blackberries
3   mangoes, peeled and cut into ¾-inch (2 cm) pieces (about
      3 cups/750 mL)
2   tablespoons (30 mL) fresh lime juice
¼   cup (50 mL) granulated sugar
2   teaspoons (10 mL) cornstarch

Topping: In medium bowl, combine oats, sugar, flour, salt and cinnamon. Using back of fork, cut in butter until mixture is crumbly.

Filling: In large bowl, combine blackberries, mangoes and lime juice. In small bowl, combine sugar and cornstarch; sprinkle over fruit mixture and gently stir to combine. Spread fruit mixture evenly in ungreased 8-inch (20 cm) square baking dish. Sprinkle evenly with topping.

Bake at 375 F (190 C) for 45 to 50 minutes or until mangoes are tender, covering loosely with foil during last 15 minutes of baking time.

Tips

• *Substitute 3 cups (750 mL) thinly sliced peeled apples (about 2 large) for the mangoes.*
• *Topping can be made ahead, covered and refrigerated for up to 24 hours. When ready to use, you may need to loosen the mixture with a fork.*

Makes 6 servings. PER SERVING: 538 cal, 6 g pro, 18 g fat, 93 g carb.

Raspberry Vanilla Bean Shortcake

Shortcake

4	tablespoons (60 mL) granulated sugar
1	vanilla bean
2	cups (500 mL) all-purpose flour
1	tablespoon (15 mL) baking powder
¼	teaspoon (1 mL) baking soda
½	teaspoon (2 mL) salt
½	cup (125 mL) cold butter, cut into small pieces
½	cup (125 mL) light sour cream
⅓	cup (75 mL) milk
	Milk

Filling and topping

1½	cups (375 mL) whipping cream
2	tablespoons (30 mL) light sour cream
3	cups (750 mL) raspberries
2	tablespoons (30 mL) sliced natural almonds, toasted

Shortcake: Put sugar in small bowl. With sharp knife, slit vanilla bean in half lengthwise and scrape seeds into sugar. Press mixture through fine sieve set over small bowl and stir to disperse seeds. Cut vanilla bean pieces, crosswise, in quarters and submerge in sugar. Cover bowl tightly with plastic wrap and set aside for at least 2 days or for up to 2 weeks. (When ready to use, remove vanilla bean pieces, tapping lightly on side of bowl to remove any excess sugar. Discard vanilla bean pieces.)

In large bowl, combine flour, 2 tablespoons (30 mL) vanilla sugar (reserve remaining vanilla sugar and set aside), baking powder, soda and salt. Using pastry blender or two knives, cut in butter until mixture resembles coarse crumbs.

In small bowl, whisk together sour cream and ⅓ cup (75 mL) milk; add all at once to dry mixture, stirring with fork to make a soft dough. Gather into a ball and knead 3 or 4 times on lightly floured work surface; transfer to greased 8-inch (20 cm) round cake pan and gently press to fill pan. Lightly brush dough with milk and sprinkle with 1 teaspoon (5 mL) of the reserved vanilla sugar.

Bake at 425 F (220 C) for 20 to 22 minutes or until top is golden brown and cake tester when inserted in centre comes out clean. Remove from oven and turn out of pan; let cool on rack until just warm.

Meanwhile, prepare filling and topping: In bowl, beat whipping cream, sour cream and remaining vanilla sugar until soft peaks form. *(Make ahead: Cover and refrigerate for up to 2 hours, whisking before using.)*

While shortcake is still warm, slice in half horizontally. To serve, place bottom layer of shortcake on large plate and spread with half the whipped cream mixture; top with half the raspberries. Place remaining shortcake layer over filling; spread with remaining whipped cream and top with remaining raspberries. Sprinkle with toasted almonds.

Tips

- *Vanilla beans are available at specialty food stores: Look for beans that are still moist and pliable and avoid ones that are stiff or completely dried out.*
- *Omit vanilla bean in shortcake and substitute 1 teaspoon (5 mL) pure vanilla extract. Whisk vanilla extract into sour cream-milk mixture. Use plain granulated sugar in place of vanilla sugar.*
- *For best results, don't overhandle the dough. Overmixing will result in a tough shortcake.*
- *This biscuit-type shortcake is best served warm.*

Makes 8 servings. PER SERVING: 451 cal, 6 g pro, 30 g fat, 41 g carb.

Blackberry Clafouti

3	cups (750 mL) blackberries
7	tablespoons (105 mL) granulated sugar, divided
¾	cup (175 mL) all-purpose flour
½	teaspoon (2 mL) baking powder
¼	teaspoon (1 mL) salt
3	large eggs
¾	cup (175 mL) milk
2	tablespoons (30 mL) dark rum
2	tablespoons (30 mL) butter, melted
	Icing sugar

Spread blackberries evenly in greased 10-inch (25 cm) glass pie plate. Sprinkle evenly with 4 tablespoons (60 mL) granulated sugar.

In large bowl, combine flour, remaining 3 tablespoons (45 mL) granulated sugar, baking powder and salt. In medium bowl, whisk eggs and milk together. Add milk mixture to flour mixture; whisk until thoroughly blended. Stir in rum and butter. Pour batter evenly over blackberries.

Bake at 375 F (190 C) for 25 to 30 minutes or until top is puffed and golden and edges are lightly browned. Let clafouti cool slightly in pie plate on rack, about 10 minutes.

Dust clafouti generously with icing sugar. Cut in wedges and serve warm.

Tips

• *To dust this French country-style dessert with icing sugar, place sugar in small sieve and hold over clafouti; lightly tap edge of sieve to distribute sugar evenly over top of dessert.*
• *Frozen black berries can be substituted for fresh. Measure frozen berries; place in colander to completely thaw. Spread thawed berries on paper towel to absorb excess moisture before using.*

Makes 6 servings. PER SERVING: 263 cal, 6 g pro, 7 g fat, 41 g carb.

Tropical Carrot and Pineapple Cupcakes

Cupcakes

3	cups (750 mL) all-purpose flour
1½	teaspoons (7 mL) baking soda
½	teaspoon (2 mL) salt
1½	teaspoons (7 mL) ground cinnamon
1	cup (250 mL) granulated sugar
½	cup (125 mL) vegetable oil
2	teaspoons (10 mL) pure vanilla extract
2	large eggs
1	(398 mL) can crushed pineapple packed in its own juice
2½	cups (625 mL) finely grated carrots
1	cup (250 mL) chopped pecans or walnuts
2	tablespoons (30 mL) finely grated orange zest

Icing

½	(250 g) package light cream cheese, softened
1	teaspoon (5 mL) pure vanilla extract
3	cups (750 mL) sifted icing sugar, about
1¼	cups (300 mL) sweetened flaked coconut

Grease 18 (2¾-inch in diameter by 1¼-inch deep/7 cm x 3 cm) muffin cups or line with paper cups.

Cupcakes: In large bowl, combine flour, soda, salt and cinnamon. In another large bowl, combine sugar, oil and vanilla; beat well. Add eggs, one at a time, beating well after each addition. Stir in pineapple with juice, carrots, pecans and zest. Stir in flour mixture, half at a time, until just combined (do not overbeat). Spoon batter into muffin cups.

Bake at 350 F (180 C) for about 20 minutes or until top of cupcake springs back when pressed lightly with fingertips. Remove cupcakes from pan and let cool completely on rack. *(Make ahead: Place cooled cupcakes in container with tight-fitting lid and store at room temperature for up to 2 days.)*

Icing: In medium bowl, beat cream cheese until smooth. Beat in vanilla. Gradually beat in sugar until of spreading consistency. Put coconut on plate.

Spread each cupcake with about 4 teaspoons (20 mL) of icing, then gently dip top into coconut to coat; sprinkle with extra coconut, if desired. Serve immediately or store in the fridge in a container with a tight-fitting lid for up to 4 hours. Makes 18 cupcakes.

Variation: For mini cupcakes, spoon batter into greased 1¾-inch in diameter by 1-inch deep (4.5 cm x 2.5 cm) mini muffin pans. Bake at 350 F (180 C) for about 15 minutes. Makes 36 mini cupcakes.
PER MINI CUPCAKE: 189 cal, 3 g pro, 7 g fat, 27 g carb. (Or makes 12 regular size cupcakes and 12 mini cupcakes.)

Tips
• *Add just enough icing sugar to the icing to make a spreading consistency (an icing that's too stiff will prevent the coconut from sticking).*
• *Use an ice cream scoop to ladle the batter into the regular size muffin cups.*

Makes 18 cupcakes. PER CUPCAKE: 377 cal, 5 g pro, 14 g fat, 55 g carb.

Tomato Soup Cake

Cake

2	cups (500 mL) sifted cake flour
2½	teaspoons (12 mL) baking powder
½	teaspoon (2 mL) baking soda
½	teaspoon (2 mL) ground cinnamon
½	teaspoon (2 mL) ground nutmeg
¼	teaspoon (1 mL) ground cloves
½	cup (125 mL) shortening
1	cup (250 mL) granulated sugar
2	large eggs
1	(284 mL) can condensed tomato soup (not reconstituted)
1	cup (250 mL) raisins

Icing

1	(250 g) package cream cheese, softened
1	tablespoon (15 mL) milk
1	teaspoon (5 mL) pure vanilla extract
5	cups (1.25 L) sifted icing sugar, about

Cake: In medium bowl, combine flour, baking powder, soda, cinnamon, nutmeg and cloves. In large bowl, beat shortening until creamy. Gradually beat in sugar until fluffy. Add eggs, one at a time, beating well after each addition. Add flour mixture alternately with soup, stirring after each addition. Fold in raisins. Transfer batter to greased and floured 13x9-inch (33x23 cm) baking pan.

Bake at 350 F (180 C) for 35 minutes or until cake tester inserted in centre of cake comes out clean and centre springs back when pressed lightly with fingertips. Let cake cool completely in pan on rack.

Icing: In large bowl, beat cream cheese and milk until blended. Beat in vanilla. Gradually beat in sugar until of spreading consistency. Spread evenly over cake. *(Make ahead: Cover and refrigerate for up to 2 days.)*

Tip: *Butter can be substituted for shortening in this favourite spice cake.*

Makes 18 servings. PER SERVING: 346 cal, 3 g pro, 12 g fat, 59 g carb.

Raspberry Cake

Topping

½	cup (125 mL) packed brown sugar
1	tablespoon (15 mL) butter, at room temperature
2	tablespoons (30 mL) all-purpose flour

Cake

1	cup (250 mL) all-purpose flour
¾	cup (175 mL) granulated sugar
½	teaspoon (2 mL) baking powder
¼	teaspoon (1 mL) baking soda
¼	teaspoon (1 mL) salt
1	large egg
⅓	cup (75 mL) buttermilk
⅓	cup (75 mL) butter, melted and cooled to room temperature
½	teaspoon (2 mL) pure vanilla extract
1¼	cups (300 mL) raspberries

Topping: In small bowl, mix together sugar, butter and flour to form fine crumbs.

Cake: In large bowl, combine flour, sugar, baking powder, soda and salt. In another bowl, beat together egg, buttermilk, butter and vanilla until smooth; add to flour mixture and stir just until dry ingredients are moistened.

Spread batter evenly in greased 8-inch (20 cm) square baking pan. Place raspberries evenly on top. Sprinkle topping evenly over berries.

Bake at 375 F (190 C) for 35 to 40 minutes or until well browned. Let cake cool in pan on rack until slightly warm.

Tip: *Serve this homey raspberry cake slightly warm from the oven, topped with a dollop of vanilla ice cream.*

Makes 9 servings. PER SERVING: 260 cal, 3 g pro, 9 g fat, 44 g carb.

Cranberry Upside-Down Gingerbread

Topping

1½ cups (375 mL) cranberries
1   small orange, peeled and cut into chunks
2½ tablespoons (37 mL) butter, at room temperature
¼   cup (50 mL) maple syrup

Cake

1¼ cups (300 mL) all-purpose flour
¾   teaspoon (4 mL) baking soda
½   teaspoon (2 mL) salt
1   teaspoon (5 mL) ground cinnamon
½   teaspoon (2 mL) ground ginger
¼   teaspoon (1 mL) ground cloves
½   cup (125 mL) buttermilk
¼   cup (50 mL) butter, at room temperature
¼   cup (50 mL) granulated sugar
1   large egg
½   cup (125 mL) fancy molasses
2   tablespoons (30 mL) finely chopped, drained preserved ginger
    Whipped cream, optional

Topping: In food processor, pulse cranberries and orange until coarsely chopped. Melt butter in 8-inch (20 cm) square baking dish in 350 F (180 C) oven. Pour maple syrup evenly over butter. Spoon cranberry mixture evenly over butter and maple syrup.

Cake: In large bowl, combine flour, soda, salt, cinnamon, ground ginger and cloves. In blender, combine buttermilk, butter, sugar, egg and molasses; process until smooth. Add preserved ginger and process to mix; stir into flour mixture. Pour over cranberry mixture; spread evenly. Bake at 350 F (180 C) for 40 to 45 minutes or until centre springs back when pressed lightly with fingertips, covering loosely with foil during last 10 minutes of baking time. Loosen cake from edge of dish; immediately invert onto heatproof serving plate. Serve warm with whipped cream.

Makes 9 servings. PER SERVING: 255 cal, 3 g pro, 9 g fat, 43 g carb.

Grand Marnier Pineapple Carrot Cake

Cake

1	(227 mL) can crushed pineapple packed in its own juice
2¼	cups (550 mL) all-purpose flour
2	teaspoons (10 mL) baking powder
¾	teaspoon (4 mL) baking soda
¾	teaspoon (4 mL) salt
1	teaspoon (5 mL) ground cinnamon
1¼	cups (300 mL) granulated sugar
¾	cup (175 mL) vegetable oil
1	teaspoon (5 mL) pure vanilla extract
3	large eggs
⅓	cup (75 mL) Grand Marnier
2	cups (500 mL) finely grated carrots
2	tablespoons (30 mL) finely grated orange zest

Icing

½	(250 g) package cream cheese, softened
¼	cup (50 mL) butter, at room temperature
2	tablespoons (30 mL) sour cream
1	teaspoon (5 mL) pure vanilla extract
3	cups (750 mL) sifted icing sugar, about
½	cup (125 mL) sliced natural almonds, toasted (optional)

Cake: Put crushed pineapple in sieve and let drain, stirring and pressing pineapple with back of spoon to remove excess juice (save juice for another use).

In large bowl, combine flour, baking powder, soda, salt and cinnamon. In another large bowl, whisk together sugar, oil and vanilla. Add eggs, one at a time, whisking well after each addition. Whisk in Grand Marnier. Stir in drained pineapple, carrots and zest until blended. Make a well in flour mixture; add oil mixture and stir just until dry ingredients are moistened. Transfer batter to greased 13x9-inch (33x23 cm) baking pan.

Bake at 350 F (180 C) for 30 to 35 minutes or until cake tester inserted in centre of cake comes out clean and centre springs back when pressed lightly with fingertips. Let cake cool in pan on rack.

Icing: In large bowl, beat cream cheese, butter and sour cream until smooth. Beat in vanilla. Beat in sugar, one-third at a time, until of spreading consistency. Spread icing over top of cake. Sprinkle almonds evenly over icing. *(Make ahead: Cover and refrigerate for up to 2 days.)*

Variation: Omit Grand Marnier and use ⅓ cup (75 mL) pineapple juice drained from crushed pineapple. Increase vanilla extract to 2 teaspoons (10 mL). Increase baking soda to 1 teaspoon (5 mL). Increase cinnamon to 1½ teaspoons (7 mL).

Tips

• *If you can't find a 227-mL can of crushed pineapple buy a 398-mL can. Drain in sieve, stirring and pressing pineapple with back of spoon to remove excess juice. Measure ¾ cup (175 mL) lightly packed, drained pineapple for recipe (save remaining pineapple and juice for another use).*

• *This leaner version of the classic carrot cake, spiked with Grand Marnier, received excellent reviews from taste testers. This new version has 223 fewer calories, 18 fewer grams of fat and 17 fewer grams of carbohydrate per piece.*

• *The Grand Marnier Pineapple Carrot Cake is moist enough to eat on its own. Without the icing, each piece of cake has 105 fewer calories, 5 fewer grams of fat and 15 fewer grams of carbohydrate.*

Makes 18 servings. PER SERVING: 339 cal, 4 g pro, 15 g fat, 47 g carb.

Upside-Down Pear Skillet Cake

Topping

⅓   cup (75 mL) buttor, at room temperature
⅓   cup (75 mL) packed brown sugar
6   pears, cored, peeled and halved (about)
3   tablespoons (45 mL) fresh orange juice
3   tablespoons (45 mL) finely chopped crystallized ginger
½   cup (125 mL) pecan halves

Cake

¾   cup (175 mL) butter, at room temperature
½   cup (125 mL) granulated sugar
1   teaspoon (5 mL) pure vanilla extract
2   large eggs
¾   cup (175 mL) sour cream
1   tablespoon (15 mL) finely grated orange zest
1½   cups (375 mL) all-purpose flour
1   tablespoon (15 mL) ground almonds
1   teaspoon (5 mL) baking powder
½   teaspoon (2 mL) baking soda
½   teaspoon (2 mL) salt

Topping: In heavy 12-inch (30 cm) non-stick ovenproof frypan, melt butter; remove from heat. Sprinkle sugar over butter. Arrange pear halves, cut side down, in frypan; sprinkle with juice, ginger and pecans.

Cake: In large bowl, beat butter, sugar and vanilla until fluffy. Beat in eggs, one at a time, beating well after each addition. Stir in sour cream and zest; mix well. In small bowl, combine flour, almonds, baking powder, soda and salt; add to sour cream mixture and stir just until combined. Spread batter evenly over pears.

Bake at 350 F (180 C) for 40 to 45 minutes or until golden and cake tester inserted into centre of cake comes out clean. Let stand in pan on rack for 10 minutes. Loosen cake from edge of pan and invert onto heatproof serving plate. Serve warm.

Makes 8 servings. PER SERVING: 536 cal, 6 g pro, 35 g fat, 53 g carb.

Santiago Almond Torte

1½   cups (375 mL) whole blanched almonds
1   cup (250 mL) granulated sugar, divided
½   cup (125 mL) butter, at room temperature
4   teaspoons (20 mL) finely grated lemon zest
4   large eggs
½   cup (125 mL) water, at room temperature
2   tablespoons (30 mL) Spanish brandy
1   cup (250 mL) all-purpose flour
½   teaspoon (2 mL) salt
     Icing sugar

In food processor, process almonds and ¼ cup (50 mL) granulated sugar until finely ground. In large bowl, beat butter and remaining ¾ cup (175 mL) granulated sugar until fluffy. Beat in zest. Add eggs, one at a time, beating well after each addition. Stir in water and brandy. Stir in flour and salt until blended. (Batter will curdle.) Fold in almond mixture; pour into greased and floured 9½-inch (24 cm) springform pan.

Bake at 350 F (180 C) for about 45 minutes or until cake tester inserted in centre of cake comes out clean and centre springs back when pressed lightly with fingertips. Run knife around edge of cake and remove side of pan; let cake stand on base on rack until completely cool.

Dust cake with icing sugar, or place a template of a cross on centre of cake and sprinkle with icing sugar. Remove template; put cake on platter.

Tips
• *This recipe is adapted from one in The Spanish Table, by Marimar Torres, published by Doubleday & Company, Inc., 1986. We used a Spanish brandy, called Fundador Brandy de Jerez, but you can substitute your favourite brandy.*
• *Simple and not-too-sweet, this cake is perfect with a glass of fine sherry or a wedge of manchego cheese and fresh fruit.*

Makes 12 servings. PER SERVING: 326 cal, 7 g pro, 20 g fat, 32 g carb.

Irish Apple Cake

Filling

3	Golden Delicious or Spartan apples
1	tablespoon (15 mL) fresh lemon juice
¼	cup (50 mL) raisins
¼	teaspoon (1 mL) ground allspice
¼	teaspoon (1 mL) ground cinnamon
¼	teaspoon (1 mL) ground nutmeg
	Pinch ground cloves
1	tablespoon (15 mL) liquid honey

Cake

2	cups (500 mL) all-purpose flour
1	teaspoon (5 mL) baking powder
½	cup (125 mL) cold butter, cut into ¼-inch (5 mm) cubes
½	cup (125 mL) packed brown sugar
1	large egg
¼	cup (50 mL) milk

Garnish

1	cup (250 mL) whipping cream, whipped
2	tablespoons (30 mL) packed brown sugar

Filling: Peel and core apples; cut into ½-inch (1 cm) thick slices. (You should have about 3 cups/750 mL.) In large bowl, toss apples with lemon juice, raisins, allspice, cinnamon, nutmeg and cloves. Add honey and mix thoroughly.

Cake: In large bowl, combine flour and baking powder. Using pastry blender or two knives, cut in butter until mixture resembles coarse crumbs. Stir in sugar. Make well in centre; combine egg and milk, and pour into well. Using fork or hands, mix to form soft, sticky dough; divide dough in half.

Using floured fingers, gently pat one portion of the dough onto bottom and 1 inch (2.5 cm) up side of greased 9-inch (23 cm) pie plate. Spoon filling evenly over dough. Lightly press small pieces of remaining dough between fingertips and place on top of filling. (Dough will not cover top completely, some parts of apples will be showing.) Press side edges and top of dough together.

Bake at 350 F (180 C) for 35 to 40 minutes or until cake is golden and firm to the touch. Cut into wedges while hot. Serve warm.

Garnish: Top each wedge with an equal portion of whipped cream and a sprinkling of sugar.

Tip: This rustic warm Irish dessert recipe was adapted by Ruth Phelan when she returned to Canada after working many years ago at The Ballymaloe Cookery School in southwest Ireland, where she learned not to overwork the dough. Minimal handling will produce a tender biscuit-like texture.

Makes 8 servings. PER SERVING: 448 cal, 5 g pro, 23 g fat, 57 g carb.

Baked Lemon Cake Pudding

1½   cups (375 mL) granulated sugar
6   tablespoons (90 mL) all-purpose flour
¼   teaspoon (1 mL) salt
1   tablespoon (15 mL) finely grated lemon zest
6   tablespoons (90 mL) fresh lemon juice
3   large eggs, separated
1½   cups (375 mL) milk

In large bowl, combine sugar, flour and salt. In medium bowl, whisk together lemon zest and juice, egg yolks and milk; whisk into flour mixture.

In medium bowl, beat egg whites until stiff, glossy peaks form; fold into lemon mixture.

Pour batter into greased 8-inch (20 cm) square baking dish. Put in larger pan and add hot water to come halfway up sides of baking dish.

Bake at 350 F (180 C) for 45 to 50 minutes or until set and lightly browned.

Tips

• *This favourite dessert of the '40s forms a lovely lemon sauce layer on the bottom and a light sponge-like cake layer on top. It's delicious served hot or cold.*

• *One large lemon yields about 4 teaspoons (20 mL) finely grated lemon zest and 4 tablespoons (60 mL) fresh lemon juice.*

Makes 6 servings. PER SERVING: 304 cal, 6 g pro, 4 g fat, 63 g carb.

Fatal Attraction Brownie Wedges with Silky Chocolate Kahlua Sauce

Brownies

4	ounces (125 g) bittersweet chocolate, chopped
½	cup (125 mL) butter, at room temperature
⅔	cup (150 mL) all-purpose flour
⅛	teaspoon (0.5 mL) salt
2	large eggs
¾	cup (175 mL) granulated sugar
1	teaspoon (5 mL) pure vanilla extract
¾	cup (175 mL) hazelnuts, toasted and chopped coarse
2	ounces (60 g) semi-sweet chocolate, chopped coarse

Sauce

¾	cup (175 mL) whipping cream
½	cup (125 mL) granulated sugar
4	ounces (125 g) semi-sweet chocolate, chopped
2	tablespoons (30 mL) butter, at room temperature
¼	teaspoon (1 mL) salt
1	tablespoon (15 mL) Kahlua, kirsch or Grand Marnier, optional

Other ingredient

3	cups (750 mL) vanilla ice cream

Brownies: Melt bittersweet chocolate with butter; let cool slightly.

In small bowl, combine flour and salt. In large bowl, beat eggs for about 2 minutes or until light and frothy. Gradually beat in sugar; beat in vanilla. Beat in melted chocolate mixture. Fold in flour mixture until not quite incorporated. Add hazelnuts and semi-sweet chocolate; fold until just incorporated. Transfer batter to lightly greased 9-inch (23 cm) springform pan; smooth top.

Bake at 350 F (180 C) for 30 minutes or until top is dry but a cake tester inserted in centre comes out with some traces of melted chocolate and moist crumbs. Place on rack and cool completely in pan. Run knife around edge of brownie and remove side of pan. *(Make ahead: Cover cooled brownie tightly with plastic wrap and refrigerate for up to 2 days. To serve, remove from refrigerator and let stand, covered, for at least 1 hour or until it reaches room temperature.)*

Sauce: In small saucepan, combine cream and sugar. Place over medium heat and bring just to a boil, stirring constantly until sugar dissolves. Reduce heat and simmer for 4 minutes, stirring frequently. Remove from heat and add chocolate, butter and salt; stir until chocolate melts. Stir in Kahlua. Let cool to room temperature. Makes 1¼ cups (300 mL). *(Make ahead: Put cooled sauce in microwaveable bowl. Cover tightly with plastic wrap and refrigerate for up to 3 days. To reheat, microwave, uncovered, on High for about 45 seconds or until mixture returns to sauce consistency, stirring every 15 seconds.)*

To serve, cut brownie into 8 wedges. Top each wedge with a scoop of ice cream and drizzle with about 2½ tablespoons (37 mL) chocolate sauce.

Tips

• *One (100 g) package hazelnuts yields ¾ cup (175 mL).*
• *Time-saver: In a pinch, substitute a commercial brownie mix for our brownie recipe (following package instructions and using their pan size).*

Makes 8 servings. PER SERVING: 770 cal, 9 g pro, 53 g fat, 76 g carb.

Dark Mocha Fondue

¾   cup (175 mL) whipping cream
¼   teaspoon (1 mL) instant coffee powder
¾   pound (350 g) semi-sweet chocolate, chopped
1   tablespoon (15 mL) Grand Marnier
4   cups (1 L) bite-size pieces fresh fruit (combination of kiwifruit
     wedges, pineapple chunks, strawberries, or other fruit)

In top of double boiler, combine cream, coffee powder and chocolate.
Place over hot, not simmering water and stir constantly until three-
quarters of the chocolate has melted. Remove from heat and stir until
chocolate has completely melted. Stir in Grand Marnier. Transfer
immediately to fondue pot; set over fondue burner. Serve immediately.

To serve, arrange fruit on platter or on each of 4 individual serving plates.
Spear fruit piece with fondue fork and dip into chocolate; remove from
fork into dessert bowl and eat with regular fork.

Tips

• Be sure and buy premium chocolate, as it will make a big difference in
the flavour and texture of your fondue.
• To prevent sauce from thinning, use paper towels to pat any excess
moisture from fruit.
• In addition to fruit, include some pieces of pound or sponge cake for
dipping.
• If you don't have a double boiler, put chocolate mixture in medium-size
heavy saucepan and place over very low heat, stirring constantly until
three-quarters of the chocolate has melted. Remove from heat; stir until
chocolate is completely melted.

Makes 4 servings. PER SERVING: 705 cal, 6 g pro, 46 g fat, 80 g carb.

Barbecued Peaches with Ginger Honey Baste

2	tablespoons (30 mL) liquid honey
1	tablespoon (15 mL) butter, melted
2	teaspoons (10 mL) fresh lemon juice
1	teaspoon (5 mL) ground ginger
4	peaches, peeled, halved and pitted
	Vanilla ice cream

In small bowl, whisk together honey, butter, lemon juice and ginger.

Lightly brush honey mixture over peach halves. Place peaches on greased barbecue grill over medium-high heat and cook for 8 to 12 minutes or until hot and lightly browned, turning frequently and brushing lightly with honey mixture. Serve warm peaches topped with ice cream.

Tip: *For easy peeling, blanch peaches by dropping into boiling water for about 30 seconds, then cool immediately in ice cold water.*

Makes 4 servings. PER SERVING: 96 cal, 1 g pro, 3 g fat, 19 g carb.

Strawberry Tart with Creamy Lime Filling (recipe on following page)

From the Fridge

Strawberry Tart
with Creamy Lime Filling

Yogurt cheese

1	cup (250 mL) low-fat plain yogurt (see tip)

Filling

2	large eggs
2	large egg yolks
¾	cup (175 mL) granulated sugar
1	teaspoon (5 mL) finely grated lime zest
¼	cup (50 mL) fresh lime juice
¼	cup (50 mL) butter, at room temperature
¼	cup (50 mL) whipping cream
2	tablespoons (30 mL) icing sugar

Pastry

⅓	cup (75 mL) hazelnuts, toasted
2	tablespoons (30 mL) icing sugar
1¼	cups (300 mL) all-purpose flour
½	teaspoon (2 mL) salt
½	cup (125 mL) butter, at room temperature
1	large egg yolk, lightly beaten
2	ounces (60 g) semi-sweet chocolate, chopped
1	teaspoon (5 mL) butter, at room temperature

Topping

3	cups (750 mL) strawberries, sliced
1	tablespoon (15 mL) red currant jelly
¾	teaspoon (4 mL) fresh lemon juice

Yogurt cheese: Place yogurt in cheesecloth-lined sieve set over bowl. Cover tightly and let drain in refrigerator overnight. Discard liquid.

Filling: In large microwaveable bowl, whisk together whole eggs, egg yolks and granulated sugar. Whisk in lime zest and juice, and butter (butter will not blend completely). Microwave on High for 1 minute; whisk until smooth. Microwave on High for 2½ minutes or until mixture boils and thickens slightly. Whisk until smooth; let cool slightly. Cover surface with plastic wrap and refrigerate for 4 hours or until completely chilled.

In small bowl, whip cream and icing sugar until stiff peaks form. Fold yogurt cheese into chilled lime mixture, then fold in whipped cream. Cover tightly and refrigerate overnight.

Pastry: In food processor, process hazelnuts and sugar until nuts are finely ground. Add flour and salt; process until well combined. Add ½ cup (125 mL) butter, in small pieces, and pulse until mixture resembles coarse crumbs. Add egg yolk; process until crumbly. Press dough evenly onto bottom and up side of 9-inch (23 cm) fluted tart pan with removable bottom. Put in freezer for 30 minutes.

Prick bottom of pastry all over with tines of fork. Bake at 400 F (200 C) for 12 to 15 minutes or until pale golden. Let cool in pan on rack.

Melt chocolate with 1 teaspoon (5 mL) butter. Brush over bottom and about a quarter of the way up side of pastry shell; let stand until chocolate is set. *(Make ahead: Pastry shell can stand overnight at room temperature.)*

Gently stir lime filling, spread evenly in prepared shell. Remove side of tart pan.

Topping: Starting at edge, arrange strawberries in concentric circles, in overlapping rows on top of filling. In small microwaveable bowl, combine jelly and lemon juice. Microwave on High for 30 seconds. Let stand for 5 minutes or until slightly thickened. Using small brush, lightly coat berries with jelly mixture. Refrigerate tart for up to 1 hour.

Tips

• *Be sure to use natural yogurt; those with added gelatin, pectin, cornstarch or carrageenan may not work.*
• *Don't be intimidated by the length of this scrumptious, five-star recipe. It's actually very easy, and all the steps can be made ahead.*

Makes 6 servings. PER SERVING: 652 cal, 11 g pro, 40 g fat, 68 g carb.

Chocolate Glazed Strawberry Tart

Pastry

½	cup (125 mL) hazelnuts, toasted
3	tablespoons (45 mL) granulated sugar
1¼	cups (300 mL) all-purpose flour
½	teaspoon (2 mL) salt
6	tablespoons (90 mL) cold butter, cut into small pieces
1	large egg, beaten
2	ounces (60 g) semi-sweet chocolate, chopped
1	teaspoon (5 mL) butter, at room temperature

Filling

¼	cup (50 mL) red currant jelly
½	teaspoon (2 mL) finely grated lemon zest
½	teaspoon (2 mL) fresh lemon juice
2	cups (500 mL) sliced strawberries
6	cups (1.5 L) small whole strawberries, about
2	ounces (60 g) semi-sweet chocolate, chopped
1	teaspoon (5 mL) butter
	Icing sugar

Pastry: In food processor, process hazelnuts and sugar until nuts are finely ground. Add flour and salt; process until well combined. Transfer to large bowl. Add 6 tablespoons (90 mL) butter; using fingertips work in butter until mixture resembles coarse crumbs. Using fork, stir in egg. (Do not overwork — mixture should be crumbly.) Press dough evenly onto bottom and up side of 10-inch (25 cm) fluted tart pan with removable bottom. Refrigerate for 30 minutes.

Prick bottom of pastry all over with tines of fork. Line pastry with foil and fill with dried beans. Bake at 350 F (180 C) for 15 minutes; remove foil and beans. Bake an additional 10 minutes or until pale golden. Let cool in pan on rack.

Melt chocolate with 1 teaspoon (5 mL) butter; brush over bottom and about a third of the way up side of pastry shell; let stand until chocolate is set. *(Make ahead: Pastry shell can stand overnight at room temperature.)*

Filling: In small saucepan, combine jelly, and lemon zest and juice. Place over low heat and stir constantly until jelly melts.

Place sliced berries evenly over chocolate-coated shell. Remove side of tart pan. Arrange whole berries, pointed side up, in single layer, on top of sliced berries. Brush with jelly mixture.

Melt chocolate with butter; drizzle over strawberries. Refrigerate until chocolate sets or for up to 2 hours. Dust with sugar before serving.

Tip: *This dessert is quite easy to make. Make the pastry shell ahead of time and all there's left to do is brush the shell with melted chocolate and fill with fresh strawberries. Give the berries a quick brush with melted jelly, a drizzle of chocolate and this eye-catching dessert is ready to serve. We recommend adding the berries no more than about 2 hours before serving to ensure the crust doesn't get soggy.*

Makes 8 servings. PER SERVING: 384 cal, 6 g pro, 22 g fat, 45 g carb.

Springtime Pavlova with Vanilla Bean Seed Whipped Cream

Meringue
4	large egg whites
½	teaspoon (2 mL) cream of tartar
1	cup (250 mL) berry (extra fine granulated) sugar
1	tablespoon (15 mL) cornstarch

Filling
1¼	cups (300 mL) whipping cream
1	vanilla bean
1	tablespoon (15 mL) icing sugar
1	cup (250 mL) sliced strawberries
1	kiwifruit, peeled, cut in half lengthwise, then slice halves crosswise
1	small mango, diced
1	ounce (30 g) dark chocolate, melted (optional)

Meringue: Line rimless baking sheet with parchment paper; trace an 8 ½-inch (21 cm) circle on paper, turn paper over.

In large glass or stainless steel bowl (don't use plastic), beat egg whites on medium-low speed until foamy. Add cream of tartar and beat on medium-high speed until soft peaks form (the peaks will fall over when the beaters are pulled out of the beaten egg whites). On high speed, gradually beat in sugar, sprinkling 1 tablespoon (15 mL) at a time over egg whites, until stiff (but not dry) glossy peaks form, about 5 minutes (peaks will stand upright when you pull the beaters out of the beaten egg whites). Sprinkle cornstarch over top and beat in.

Spread meringue onto prepared circle, mounding it up slightly around edge to create a 6-inch (15 cm) shallow depression in centre. Bake at 250 F (120 C) for 1½ hours or until crisp and dry. Turn oven off and let meringue cool in oven overnight or for 4 hours or until completely cool. With long metal spatula, loosen meringue from paper and place on serving plate. *(Make ahead: Meringue can be stored in airtight container in a cool dry place for up to 1 day.)*

Filling: Put cream in large bowl. With sharp knife, slit vanilla bean in half lengthwise and scrape seeds into cream; add vanilla bean halves. Cover bowl tightly and refrigerate overnight.

When ready to serve, remove cream-vanilla seed mixture from fridge; remove and discard vanilla bean halves. Add sugar to cream mixture and beat until soft peaks form. Spoon into meringue hollow and top with fruit. Using fork, drizzle chocolate over dessert. Refrigerate for up to 1 hour.

Tips

- *To melt chocolate, chop chocolate and put in small microwaveable bowl. Microwave on Medium for 1½ to 2 minutes; stir.*
- *Even a trace of egg yolk (which is fat) can prevent whites from beating into a foam. To avoid getting any yolk into whites, separate eggs, one at a time, dropping egg white into small bowl and yolk into another (save yolks for another use). If yolk doesn't break, transfer egg white to clean mixing bowl. (A scrupulously clean bowl and beaters are a must — a slight fat residue left in bowl can ruin your egg white foam.)*
- *Once you start to beat the egg whites, continue beating until you have finished adding the sugar and cornstarch, and the mixture forms stiff peaks. Don't stop in the middle of the beating and take a break — the partially whipped egg whites will start deflating after a few minutes.*
- *Cream of tartar is a fine white powder available in the spice section of supermarkets. It is an acid ingredient that helps to stabilize and increase the volume of beaten egg whites. Although we prefer to use cream of tartar, you could use 1 teaspoon (5 mL) pure white vinegar in place of the ½ teaspoon (2 mL) cream of tartar.*
- *Berry sugar dissolves more easily than regular granulated sugar in beaten egg whites but you can still make a good meringue substituting granulated sugar for berry sugar.*
- *Break down the preparation of this elegant dessert over a couple of days. The day before you're planning to serve this dessert, bake the meringue and add the vanilla bean seeds to the whipping cream. Just before serving, beat the whipping cream and assemble the dessert.*

Makes 8 servings. PER SERVING: 260 cal, 3 g pro, 12 g fat, 36 g carb.

Pretty-in-Pink Rhubarb Fool

2½	cups (625 mL) low-fat plain yogurt (see tip)
5	cups (1.25 L) sliced (½-inch/1 cm pieces) rhubarb
3	tablespoons (45 mL) fresh orange juice
½	cup (125 mL) granulated sugar
	Pinch salt
½	cup (125 mL) whipping cream
2	tablespoons (30 mL) granulated sugar
	Fresh mint leaves

Put yogurt in cheesecloth-lined sieve set over bowl. Cover tightly and let drain in refrigerator overnight. Discard liquid.

In large heavy non-reactive saucepan, combine rhubarb, orange juice, ½ cup (125 mL) sugar and salt. Place over medium heat and bring to a simmer, stirring until sugar is dissolved. Reduce heat to medium-low and simmer, uncovered, for 7 to 10 minutes or until rhubarb is tender, stirring occasionally. Transfer rhubarb to bowl and let cool. Cover tightly and refrigerate overnight or until cold, about 3 hours.

In medium bowl, beat cream and 2 tablespoons (30 mL) sugar until stiff. Add drained yogurt and whisk to blend; fold into chilled rhubarb mixture. *(Make ahead: Cover mixture tightly and refrigerate for up to 6 hours.)*

To serve, gently stir rhubarb mixture; spoon into 4 (about 1 cup/250 mL) parfait or wine glasses. Garnish each with mint.

Tips

• *For Ginger Rhubarb Fool, add 1 tablespoon (15 mL) chopped crystallized ginger to rhubarb mixture before cooking.*
• *For best colour, choose dark red rhubarb stalks. You'll need about 1½ pounds (750 g) to yield 5 cups (1.25 L) sliced rhubarb.*
• *Be sure to use natural yogurt; those with added gelatin, pectin, cornstarch or carrageenan may not work.*

Makes 4 servings. PER SERVING: 367 cal, 11 g pro, 13 g fat, 55 g carb.

Luscious Lemon Tart

Pastry

1¾   cups (425 mL) all-purpose flour
¼   cup (50 mL) finely chopped almonds
1   tablespoon (15 mL) granulated sugar
½   teaspoon (2 mL) salt
¾   cup (175 mL) plus 2 tablespoons (30 mL) butter, at room
        temperature

Filling

4   large eggs
4   large egg yolks
1½   cups (375 mL) granulated sugar
4   teaspoons (20 mL) finely grated lemon zest
¾   cup (175 mL) fresh lemon juice
½   cup (125 mL) butter, at room temperature
1   cup (250 mL) whipping cream, whipped
        Fresh mint leaves

Pastry: In food processor, combine flour, almonds, sugar and salt; pulse to mix. Add butter, in small pieces; pulse until mixture just starts to clump together. Press dough evenly onto bottom and up side of 10-inch (25 cm) fluted tart pan with removable bottom. Put in freezer for 30 minutes. Prick bottom of pastry all over with tines of fork. Bake at 350 F (180 C) for 25 to 30 minutes or until pale golden. Let cool in pan on rack.

Filling: In 8-cup (2 L) microwaveable bowl, whisk together whole eggs, egg yolks and sugar. Whisk in lemon zest and juice, and butter (butter will not blend in completely). Microwave on High for 1½ minutes; whisk until smooth. Microwave on High for about 6 minutes or until mixture boils and thickens slightly, whisking every 2 minutes. Whisk until smooth; let cool slightly. Cover surface with plastic wrap and refrigerate for 4 hours or until completely chilled. Spread filling evenly in pastry shell; cover and refrigerate overnight. To serve, pipe cream around outside edge; garnish with mint. (Refrigerate for up to 2 hours.)

Makes 8 servings. PER SERVING: 737 cal, 9 g pro, 50 g fat, 66 g carb.

Sliced Orange Duet
with Grand Marnier

3	small navel oranges
3	small blood oranges
⅓	cup (75 mL) maple syrup
1	tablespoon (15 mL) Grand Marnier
1	teaspoon (5 mL) fresh lemon juice
1	cinnamon stick, broken into pieces
	Fresh mint leaves

Peel navel and blood oranges, removing white pith. Cut oranges in half lengthwise and slice into ¼-inch (5 mm) thick half-rounds; put in medium bowl.

In small bowl, whisk together maple syrup, Grand Marnier and lemon juice. Pour over oranges, tossing gently to coat. Put cinnamon pieces in and around orange slices. Let stand for 1 hour at room temperature, or cover and refrigerate overnight (syrup mixture will turn red overnight), stirring occasionally. Remove cinnamon pieces and discard. Garnish each serving with mint.

Tip: If you don't want to use alcohol, substitute fresh orange juice for the Grand Marnier.

Makes 4 servings. PER SERVING: 173 cal, 3 g pro, 0 g fat, 55 g carb.

Lemon Meringue Tart

Pastry

2	tablespoons (30 mL) granulated sugar
2	teaspoons (10 mL) finely grated lemon zest
1¾	cups (425 mL) all-purpose flour
¾	teaspoon (4 mL) salt
¾	cup (175 mL) plus 2 tablespoons (30 mL) butter, at room temperature

Filling

4	large egg yolks
1¼	cups (300 mL) granulated sugar
¼	cup (50 mL) plus 2 tablespoons (30 mL) cornstarch
2	cups (500 mL) cold water
3	tablespoons (45 mL) butter, at room temperature
1	tablespoon (15 mL) finely grated lemon zest
½	cup (125 mL) fresh lemon juice, lukewarm
½	teaspoon (2 mL) salt
½	teaspoon (2 mL) pure vanilla extract

Meringue

4	large egg whites
½	teaspoon (2 mL) cream of tartar
½	cup (125 mL) plus 2 tablespoons (30 mL) sifted icing sugar

Pastry: Using fork, stir together sugar and zest in small bowl. In food processor, combine flour, sugar-zest mixture and salt; pulse to mix. Add butter, in small pieces; pulse until mixture just starts to clump together. Press dough evenly onto bottom and up side of 10-inch (25 cm) fluted tart pan with removable bottom. Put in freezer for 30 minutes.

Prick bottom of pastry all over with tines of fork. Bake at 350 F (180 C) for 25 to 30 minutes or until pale golden. Let cool in pan on rack. *(Make ahead: Pastry shell can stand overnight at room temperature.)*

Filling: In small bowl, whisk egg yolks together.

In medium-size heavy saucepan (a heavy bottomed pan is important to prevent thick filling from sticking to bottom of pan), combine sugar and cornstarch until well blended. Gradually stir in water until well blended. Place over medium-high heat until mixture comes to a boil and thickens, stirring constantly. Reduce heat to medium-low and boil gently for 1 minute (mixture will be very thick), stirring constantly. Remove saucepan from heat; increase heat to medium.

Gradually whisk ½ cup (125 mL) of the hot mixture into egg yolks until smooth. Whisking vigorously, gradually pour yolk mixture into the hot mixture in saucepan. Place over medium heat and boil (mixture should come to the boil almost immediately) gently for 3 minutes, stirring constantly. Remove from heat and stir in butter, lemon zest and juice, salt and vanilla; set aside and immediately start preparing meringue.

Meringue: In large glass or stainless steel mixing bowl (don't use plastic), beat egg whites on medium speed until foamy. Beat in cream of tartar, then 1 tablespoon (15 mL) sugar; beat on medium speed until soft peaks form. Beat in remaining sugar, 1 tablespoon (15 mL) at a time. Beat on high speed until glossy stiff peaks form.

Place cooled pastry shell (still in pan) on baking sheet. Transfer hot lemon filling to pastry shell and spread evenly. Working quickly, spoon small mounds of meringue on top of hot filling around edge and in centre of tart. Using a narrow spatula or knife, push meringue gently against edge of pastry, sealing well. Then spread rest of meringue over filling forming decorative peaks. Bake at 325 F (160 C) for about 20 minutes or until pale golden. Cool on rack for 2 hours at room temperature, then refrigerate. (If necessary, use a sharp knife to loosen any meringue attached to the pan before removing the side.) Serve tart the same day it is baked.

Tip: *To warm lemon juice, zap in microwave for about 10 seconds.*

Makes 8 servings. PER SERVING: 539 cal, 6 g pro, 27 g fat, 70 g carb.

Creme Caramel

1   cup (250 mL) granulated sugar, divided
3   tablespoons (45 mL) water
2   cups (500 mL) milk
3   large eggs
3   large egg yolks
1   teaspoon (5 mL) pure vanilla extract

In small heavy saucepan over medium heat, combine ½ cup (125 mL) sugar and water. Place over medium-high heat, stirring until sugar dissolves. Reduce heat to medium and cook, without stirring, for 10 to 12 minutes or until a deep golden brown. (Once syrup starts to turn golden, gently swirl pan to ensure even browning.) Remove from heat and immediately divide among 6 (¾ cup/175 mL) custard cups, swirling to coat bottom of cups. Place cups in large baking pan and set aside while preparing custard.

In large saucepan, heat milk over medium heat until small bubbles form around edge of pan, stirring frequently. In large heatproof bowl, whisk together whole eggs, egg yolks and remaining ½ cup (125 mL) sugar. Gradually stir in hot milk. Stir in vanilla. Pour into prepared cups. Pour enough boiling water into pan to reach halfway up sides of cups.

Bake at 350 F (180 C) for 30 to 35 minutes or until knife inserted near centre comes out clean. Immediately remove custard cups from hot water. Let cool on rack for 1½ hours at room temperature, then cover and refrigerate until well chilled. To serve, gently loosen edges of custards with knife and invert onto serving plates.

Tip: *For orange variation, omit vanilla. Using vegetable peeler, remove thin strips of zest from 1 orange and add to milk before heating; strain and discard zest. Stir 1½ tablespoons (22 mL) Grand Marnier into milk.*

Makes 6 servings. PER SERVING: 244 cal, 7 g pro, 7 g fat, 39 g carb.

Low-Fat Vanilla Rice Pudding with Dried Cranberries

6   cups (1.5 L) milk
⅔   cup (150 mL) granulated sugar
½   vanilla bean, about 4-inch (10 cm) piece
¾   cup (175 mL) short grain rice
½   cup (125 mL) dried cranberries or raisins
¼   teaspoon (1 mL) salt

In 4-quart (4 L) heavy saucepan, combine milk and sugar. With sharp knife, slit vanilla bean in half lengthwise and scrape seeds into milk mixture; add vanilla bean pieces. Place over medium-high heat and bring just to a boil, stirring occasionally. Stir in rice; return to a boil. Reduce heat to low; cover and simmer for 1¼ hours or until very creamy and slightly thickened, stirring occasionally. (Pudding thickens as it cools.)

Remove pan from heat; discard vanilla bean pieces. Stir in cranberries and salt. Transfer to large bowl and cool slightly. Cover tightly with plastic wrap and refrigerate for at least 6 hours or for up to 3 days.

Tips

• Substitute 2 teaspoons (10 mL) pure vanilla extract for vanilla bean; add to milk and sugar in saucepan before bringing to a boil.
• Trying to lower your fat intake? Make the pudding with skim milk — the texture isn't quite as creamy, but the flavour is still divine.
• Short grain rice gives the best results — a thick, creamy consistency. The pudding made from regular long grain rice isn't quite as creamy but is certainly acceptable. Skip using parboiled rice (converted rice) — we found it made a ho-hum pudding that was too thin and sloppy.

Makes 12 servings. PER SERVING: 161 cal, 5 g pro, 3 g fat, 30 g carb.

White Chocolate Mousse

2   teaspoons (10 mL) grated lemon zest
2   cups (500 mL) whipping cream, divided
6   ounces (170 g) white chocolate, chopped
4   teaspoons (20 mL) Grand Marnier
½   teaspoon (2 mL) gelatin
1   tablespoon (15 mL) cold water
       Dark chocolate curls

Finely chop grated zest. In medium-size heavy saucepan, combine 1 cup (250 mL) cream, white chocolate and zest. Cook over low heat, stirring constantly, until chocolate melts and mixture is smooth. Stir in Grand Marnier, then remove from heat.

In small saucepan, sprinkle gelatin over water; let stand for 1 minute. Place over low heat and stir until gelatin dissolves. Whisk into warm chocolate mixture. Stir in remaining 1 cup (250 mL) cream until blended; pour into large bowl. Cover tightly with plastic wrap and refrigerate for several hours or until thoroughly chilled.

On medium speed, beat chocolate mixture until soft peaks form (do not overbeat). Spoon into stemmed glasses or dessert dishes. Cover each dessert tightly with plastic wrap and refrigerate until ready to serve or overnight. Just before serving, garnish with chocolate curls.

Tip: We recommend buying premium quality white chocolate.

Makes 5 servings. PER SERVING: 500 cal, 5 g pro, 43 g fat, 24 g carb.

Chocolate Espresso Cheesecake

Crust

1	(200 g) package chocolate wafers, broken into large pieces
¼	cup (50 mL) ground pecans
¼	cup (50 mL) plus 2 tablespoons (30 mL) butter, melted

Filling

¾	pound (350 g) semi-sweet chocolate, chopped
¼	cup (50 mL) butter, at room temperature
2	tablespoons (30 mL) unsweetened cocoa powder, sifted
2	teaspoons (10 mL) instant espresso coffee powder
3	(250 g) packages cream cheese, softened
1	cup (250 mL) granulated sugar
4	large eggs
1¼	cups (300 mL) sour cream
1	teaspoon (5 mL) pure vanilla extract
	White and dark chocolate curls, optional

Grease 9½ inch (24 cm) in diameter by 3 inch (7 cm) high springform pan. Set aside a roasting pan, large enough to accommodate springform pan.

Crust: In food processor, pulse wafers until fine crumbs form (about 2½ cups/625 mL). Add pecans and pulse to combine. With motor running, slowly add butter and process just until blended. Press mixture onto bottom of prepared pan. Wrap outside of pan tightly with heavy-duty aluminum foil (being careful to avoid puncturing foil). Bake at 350 F (180 C) for 8 minutes or until set. Let cool on rack.

Filling: Melt semi-sweet chocolate with butter. Whisk in cocoa powder and coffee powder (if the instant espresso coffee you bought is granular instead of a powder, rub granules between fingertips to form a powder); let cool for about 20 minutes or until at room temperature, stirring occasionally.

In large bowl, beat cream cheese until smooth. Add sugar and beat until blended. Add eggs, one at a time, beating well after each addition. Beat in chocolate mixture just until smooth. Add sour cream and vanilla; beat until blended, scraping down side of bowl.

Pour filling onto crust; smooth top with small metal spatula. Set springform pan in roasting pan (being careful to avoid puncturing foil); carefully pour enough boiling water into roasting pan to reach halfway up side of springform pan. Bake at 350 F (180 C) for 45 to 50 minutes or until set around the edge and centre is almost set but still jiggly; do not overbake — cheesecake will firm as it cools. Remove roasting pan from oven and let cheesecake cool in water bath for 15 minutes, then remove springform pan from water bath. Remove foil from pan and let cheesecake cool completely in springform pan on rack.

Cover tightly with plastic wrap and refrigerate until thoroughly chilled, at least 6 hours or overnight. *(Make ahead: Cheesecake can be refrigerated for up to 3 days or overwrapped with heavy-duty foil and frozen for up to 1 week. Thaw in refrigerator before removing trom foil.)*

To serve, let cheesecake stand at room temperature for 20 minutes; remove side of pan. With sharp warm knife, cut into wedges. Garnish with chocolate curls.

Tips
• *To cut cheesecake smoothly, hold a sharp knife under hot running water and dry with towel before cutting each wedge.*
• *For Kahlua variation, reduce coffee powder to 1 teaspoon (5 mL) and dissolve it in 3 tablespoons (45 mL) Kahlua; add with sour cream to cream cheese mixture. Increase baking time to about 55 minutes.*
• *Use a swivel-type vegetable peeler to shave chocolate into curls. Chocolate should be just slightly warm (microwave at 5-second intervals until curls can be made without crumbling).*

Makes 16 servings. PER SERVING: 384 cal, 5 g pro, 26 g fat, 36 carb.

Honey Lavender Ice Cream (recipe on following page)

From the Freezer

Honey Lavender Ice Cream

1½	cups (375 mL) milk
2	tablespoons (30 mL) chopped fresh lavender flowers (see tip)
4	strips lemon zest
4	large egg yolks
¼	cup (50 mL) granulated sugar
¼	teaspoon (1 mL) salt
2	cups (500 mL) whipping cream
3	tablespoons (45 mL) liquid honey

In large heavy saucepan, combine milk, lavender and zest. Place over medium heat until small bubbles start to form around the edge of saucepan, stirring occasionally. Remove from heat and let stand for 30 minutes. Remove and discard zest; pour mixture into medium bowl.

In large bowl, whisk together egg yolks, sugar and salt; gradually whisk in milk mixture. Whisk in cream. Return to saucepan and cook over medium-low heat for about 15 minutes or until mixture thickens enough to coat back of wooden spoon, stirring constantly (do not let boil). Pour through fine sieve into large heatproof bowl; discard lavender (see tip). Add honey and stir until blended; let cool slightly. Cover tightly with plastic wrap and refrigerate overnight or until well chilled.

Pour chilled lavender-flavoured mixture into ice cream maker and freeze according to manufacturer's directions.

Tips

• *Some varieties of lavender are intensely flavoured and imbue a perfume scent. We used the delicate, pleasant smelling, sweet English lavender.*
• *If you enjoy a hit of lavender flavour, don't strain all of the lavender; rather, leave some behind in the ice cream mixture.*

Makes 6 servings. PER SERVING: 385 cal, 6 g pro, 32 g fat, 22 g carb.

Blueberry Ice Cream

1	small orange
2	cups (500 mL) blueberries
½	cup (125 mL) granulated sugar
2	tablespoons (30 mL) water
1½	tablespoons (22 mL) fresh lemon juice
¼	teaspoon (1 mL) pure vanilla extract
	Pinch salt
1½	cups (375 mL) cream (10 per cent M.F.)

Using vegetable peeler, remove zest of orange in strips (put aside rest of orange for another use).

In large heavy saucepan, bring blueberries, sugar, water and zest to a boil, stirring frequently until sugar dissolves. Cover and boil for 5 minutes, stirring occasionally. Uncover, reduce heat and simmer for 5 minutes. Discard zest. Let cool slightly.

In blender or food processor, puree blueberry mixture in batches. Transfer puree to large heatproof bowl and whisk in lemon juice, vanilla, salt and cream. Press mixture through sieve into another bowl. Cover tightly with plastic wrap and refrigerate overnight or until well chilled.

Pour chilled blueberry mixture into ice cream maker and freeze according to manufacturer's directions.

Tips

• *The secret to this luscious blueberry ice cream lies in cooking the berries first to release their flavour.*

• *One cup (250 mL) blueberries weighs about 5 ounces (140 g).*

Makes 6 servings. PER SERVING: 198 cal, 2 g pro, 10 g fat, 28 g carb.

Frozen Raspberry Yogurt

4	cups (1 L) raspberries
½	cup (125 mL) granulated sugar, about
⅔	cup (150 mL) low-fat lemon yogurt

In food processor or blender, puree raspberries. To remove seeds, press puree through a fine sieve into large bowl. Whisk in sugar and yogurt (taste and add a little extra sugar, if necessary). Cover tightly with plastic wrap and refrigerate overnight or until well chilled.

Pour chilled raspberry mixture into ice cream maker and freeze according to manufacturer's directions.

Tip: *If you can't find lemon yogurt, substitute plain yogurt and add 1 tablespoon (15 mL) fresh lemon juice to the raspberries before pureeing.*

Makes 6 servings. PER SERVING: 123 cal, 2 g pro, 1 g fat, 29 g carb.

Mango Ice Cream

1	cup (250 mL) milk, divided
¼	cup (50 mL) plus 3 tablespoons (45 mL) granulated sugar
⅛	teaspoon (0.5 mL) salt
1	cup (250 mL) whipping cream
1½	cups (375 mL) mango puree (about 2 large, ripe mangoes)
1½	teaspoons (7 mL) pure vanilla extract

In small heavy saucepan, heat ½ cup (125 mL) milk until just lukewarm. Add sugar and salt; stir until sugar is dissolved. Stir in remaining ½ cup (125 mL) milk. Pour into bowl; cover tightly with plastic wrap and refrigerate overnight or until well chilled.

Stir cream, mango puree and vanilla into milk mixture. Pour into ice cream maker and freeze according to manufacturer's directions.

Tip: *The easiest way to remove flesh from the mango pit is to hold the fruit so the narrow side faces you, stem end up. Make one vertical cut about ½ inch (1 cm) to the right of the stem, just clearing the pit in the centre, and another ½ inch (1 cm) to the left. Score the flesh into cubes, then press the skin so the flesh pops outward. Use a paring knife to slice the cubes of flesh from the skin. Puree in blender or food processor.*

Makes 8 servings. PER SERVING: 172 cal, 2 g pro, 11 g fat, 18 g carb.

Vanilla Bean Ice Cream

2   cups (500 mL) whipping cream
1½ cups (375 mL) milk
1   vanilla bean
4   large egg yolks
¾   cup (175 mL) granulated sugar
¼   teaspoon (1 mL) salt

In large heavy saucepan, combine cream and milk. Slit vanilla bean in half lengthwise and scrape seeds into cream mixture; add vanilla bean halves. Place saucepan over medium heat until small bubbles start to form around the edge of saucepan, stirring occasionally; remove from heat. Remove vanilla bean halves and set aside.

In large bowl, whisk together egg yolks, sugar and salt; gradually whisk in hot cream mixture. Return to saucepan and cook over medium-low heat for about 15 minutes or until mixture thickens enough to coat back of wooden spoon, stirring constantly (do not let boil). Pour through fine sieve into large heatproof bowl; add reserved vanilla bean halves and cool slightly. Cover tightly with plastic wrap and refrigerate overnight or until well chilled.

Remove vanilla bean halves and discard.

Pour chilled vanilla-seed mixture into ice cream maker and freeze according to manufacturer's directions.

Tips

• *We prefer the flavour and appearance of ice cream made with a vanilla bean but we're sure no one will complain if you substitute pure vanilla extract for the bean. Omit vanilla bean and substitute 2 teaspoons (10 mL) vanilla extract. Add vanilla extract to slightly cooled custard mixture just before refrigerating.*

• *This recipe makes about 3 ½ cups (875 mL) — enough ice cream to fill 8 Jumbo Chocolate Ice Cream Sandwiches (see recipe, page 77).*

Makes 6 servings. PER SERVING: 420 cal, 6 g pro, 32 g fat, 30 g carb.

Jumbo Chocolate
Ice Cream Sandwiches

Cookies

½	pound (250 g) bittersweet chocolate, chopped
¼	cup (50 mL) all-purpose flour
½	teaspoon (2 mL) baking powder
⅛	teaspoon (0.5 mL) salt
¾	cup (175 mL) granulated sugar
2	large eggs
2	tablespoons (30 mL) butter, melted
1	teaspoon (5 mL) pure vanilla extract
1	teaspoon (5 mL) instant espresso coffee powder (see tip)
1	(100 g) white chocolate bar, chopped
½	cup (125 mL) pecan halves, toasted and chopped

Ice cream sandwiches

3½	cups (875 mL) Vanilla Bean Ice Cream (see recipe, page 75)

Cookies: Line 2 large baking sheets with parchment paper.

Melt bittersweet chocolate; let cool slightly.

In small bowl, combine flour, baking powder and salt. In large bowl, beat sugar and eggs for about 5 minutes or until pale yellow and thick. Beat in melted chocolate, butter, vanilla and coffee powder. Add flour mixture and stir just until blended. Stir in white chocolate and pecans. Let dough stand at room temperature for about 5 minutes or until slightly stiff.

Drop all the dough by scant ¼ cupfuls (3 level tablespoons/45 mL) onto prepared baking sheets then, using lightly floured fingertips, flatten each cookie into a 3-inch (7 cm) circle, spacing cookies 2 inches (5 cm) apart.

Bake at 350 F (180 C) for 10 to 12 minutes or until tops become dry and crack. (Centres should be very soft. Do not overbake.)

Let cookies cool on baking sheet on rack for 3 minutes, then transfer cookies to rack and let cool completely. Put cookies in freezer container and place in freezer overnight or until frozen. Makes 16 cookies.

Ice cream sandwiches: Put large rimmed baking sheet in freezer.

Remove container of ice cream from freezer and put in refrigerator for 20 to 30 minutes or until just slightly softened.

For each sandwich, place a generous ⅓ cup (75 mL) ice cream on centre of flat side of 1 frozen cookie; spread evenly with spatula. Top with another frozen cookie, flat side on top of ice cream; lightly press cookies together. With metal spatula, smooth ice cream around edges. Put ice cream sandwich on baking sheet in freezer and freeze for 2 hours or until ice cream is firm. *(Make ahead: Ice cream sandwiches can be stored in single layer in freezer containers or freezer plastic bags in freezer for up to 1 week. Before serving, let cookies stand at room temperature until ice cream is slightly softened.)*

Tips

• *If you're serving these decadent ice cream sandwiches for dessert after a large meal, you might want to cut them in half.*

• *Splurge and use premium quality chocolate for these cookies — besides the wonderful flavour it's easier to melt.*

• *Parchment paper prevents the chocolate in the cookies from scorching.*

• *Look for instant espresso coffee powder in specialty food stores and Italian delis. If the espresso coffee you buy is granular instead of a powder, rub granules between fingertips to form a powder. If you can't find instant espresso powder in your area, substitute a dark roast instant coffee powder.*

• *If desired, store-bought vanilla ice cream can be substituted for home-made ice cream.*

Makes 8 servings. PER SANDWICH: 708 cal, 10 g pro, 50 g fat, 67 g carb.

Vanilla Ice Cream Sundaes with Hot Silky Chocolate Sauce

½ cup (125 mL) whipping cream
¼ cup (50 mL) granulated sugar
Pinch salt
4 ounces (125 g) bittersweet chocolate, chopped
2 tablespoons (30 mL) butter, at room temperature
3 cups (750 mL) light vanilla ice cream or frozen vanilla yogurt
½ cup (125 mL) hazelnuts, toasted and chopped coarse

In small heavy saucepan, combine cream, sugar and salt; bring just to a boil over medium heat, stirring constantly until sugar dissolves. Reduce heat and simmer for 4 minutes, stirring frequently. Remove from heat; add chocolate and butter, stirring until chocolate melts. Let cool slightly. *(Make ahead: Put sauce in microwaveable bowl; cover tightly with plastic wrap and refrigerate for up to 3 days. To reheat, microwave, uncovered, on High for about 45 seconds or until mixture returns to sauce consistency, stirring every 15 seconds.)*

For each sundae: Spoon 2 tablespoons (30 mL) warm chocolate sauce into sundae dish or dessert bowl. Top with ¾ cup (175 mL) ice cream. Sprinkle with 2 tablespoons (30 mL) chopped hazelnuts. Drizzle about 2 tablespoons (30 mL) warm chocolate sauce on top.

Tip: *Make this velvety sauce even more luxurious by stirring 1 tablespoon (15 mL) Kahlua or Grand Marnier into the warm chocolate sauce.*

Makes 4 servings. PER SERVING: 692 cal, 12 g pro, 48 g fat, 65 g carb.

Bumbleberry Sundaes

5   cups (1.25 L) berries (any combination of blackberries, blueberries and raspberries), divided
3   tablespoons (45 mL) water
⅓   cup (75 mL) granulated sugar
1   tablespoon (15 mL) finely grated orange zest
3   cups (750 mL) light vanilla ice cream or frozen vanilla yogurt
2   (39 g) chocolate-covered toffee bars (such as Skor bars), chopped

In large heavy saucepan, combine 3 cups (750 mL) of the berries, water, sugar and zest; cook over medium heat for 13 to 15 minutes or until thickened and berries have broken down, stirring occasionally.

Strain mixture through fine sieve into bowl, pressing on solids. Cover tightly and refrigerate until chilled.

For each sundae: Spoon 1 tablespoon (15 mL) berry sauce into sundae dish or dessert bowl. Top with ¾ cup (175 mL) ice cream. Sprinkle with 2 tablespoons (30 mL) chopped toffee bar and ½ cup (125 mL) berries. Drizzle 2 tablespoons (30 mL) berry sauce on top.

Tip: *For a little flavour intensity, add 1 tablespoon (15 mL) of your favourite berry liqueur to the berry mixture before cooking — creme de cassis (black currant) or framboise (raspberry) are tasty choices. Alternatively, a non-alcoholic concentrated black currant nectar such as Ribena is also suitable.*

Makes 4 servings. PER SERVING: 479 cal, 8 g pro, 12 g fat, 90 g carb.

Vanilla Ice Cream Terrine with Fudgey Chocolate Sauce

Terrine

¾   cup (175 mL) hazelnuts, toasted and chopped coarse

3   (39 g) chocolate-covered toffee bars (such as Skor bars), chopped coarse

6   cups (1.5 L) vanilla ice cream

Sauce

4   ounces (125 g) semi-sweet chocolate, chopped

¼   cup (50 mL) cream (10 per cent M.F.)

⅓   cup (75 mL) golden corn syrup

3   tablespoons (45 mL) water

¼   cup (50 mL) granulated sugar

Pinch salt

3   tablespoons (45 mL) butter, at room temperature

Terrine: In medium bowl, combine hazelnuts and chopped toffee bars. Remove container of ice cream from freezer and put in refrigerator for 20 minutes. Remove 3 cups (750 mL) ice cream from container and put into large bowl; refrigerate for 10 minutes or until softened slightly, stirring occasionally. (Return ice cream container to freezer.)

Meanwhile, line bottom and sides of 9x5-inch (23x13 cm) loaf pan with 2 large overlapping pieces of plastic wrap, letting wrap hang over sides of pan. Spoon softened ice cream from bowl into loaf pan, pressing down with rubber spatula to form an even layer. Sprinkle evenly with hazelnut mixture; press lightly. Put in freezer for 20 minutes or until ice cream is slightly firm.

Meanwhile, remove ice cream container from freezer and spoon another 3 cups (750 mL) ice cream into bowl; refrigerate for 15 minutes or until softened. (Put any remaining ice cream in container back in freezer for another use.)

Remove loaf pan from freezer and spoon softened ice cream in bowl over hazelnut mixture, pressing down with rubber spatula to spread evenly. Fold overhanging ends of plastic wrap overtop of ice cream to cover. Put in freezer overnight. *(Make ahead: Overwrap with foil and freeze for up to 3 days.)*

Sauce: In small heavy saucepan, combine chocolate, cream, corn syrup, water, sugar, salt and butter; bring just to a boil over medium heat, stirring constantly. Reduce heat and boil gently for 8 to 10 minutes or until slightly thickened, stirring frequently. Let stand until slightly warm, about 20 minutes. *(Make ahead: Put cooled sauce in microwaveable bowl; cover tightly with plastic wrap and refrigerate for up to 3 days. To reheat, microwave, uncovered, on High for 1 minute or until warm, stirring every 15 seconds.)*

To serve, remove loaf pan from freezer; peel back plastic wrap and invert terrine onto cutting board. Remove and discard plastic wrap. Cut terrine into slices about ½-inch (2 cm) thick; cut each slice in half. Place 2 halves, one overlapping the other, on each dessert plate and drizzle with warm chocolate sauce.

Tips

• *Skor toffee bits are available in 200-gram packages. Although we preferred the texture and flavour of the Skor chocolate bars (the toffee bits aren't covered with chocolate), you could substitute ¾ cup (175 mL) toffee bits for the coarsely chopped chocolate bars — we're sure no one will complain.*

• *Dessert recipes don't come much easier to make than this one. The ice cream, crunchy toffee filling and chocolate sauce can all be purchased at the supermarket, leaving you with just the assembly. We prefer the dessert with our home-made chocolate sauce that can be prepared ahead of time, but if you are pressed for time, buy a favourite sauce and eliminate that step.*

Makes 14 servings. PER SERVING: 337 cal, 4 g pro, 22 g fat, 35 g carb.

Pumpkin Ice Cream Torte
with Caramel Sauce

Crust

1¼ cups (300 mL) gingersnap cookie crumbs

1 cup (250 mL) pecan halves, ground

¼ cup (50 mL) plus 3 tablespoons (45 mL) butter, melted

Filling

1 (398 mL) can pumpkin

⅔ cup (150 mL) packed brown sugar

½ teaspoon (2 mL) salt

1½ teaspoons (7 mL) ground cinnamon

½ teaspoon (2 mL) ground ginger

½ teaspoon (2 mL) ground nutmeg

¼ cup (50 mL) water

2 tablespoons (30 mL) brandy

8 cups (2 L) light vanilla ice cream

Toasted pecan halves for garnish

Sauce

1⅓ cups (325 mL) cream (10 per cent M.F.)

1½ cups (375 mL) packed brown sugar

½ cup (125 mL) granulated sugar

⅔ cup (150 mL) butter, at room temperature

1 tablespoon (15 mL) brandy

¾ cup (175 mL) pecan halves, toasted and chopped coarse (optional)

Crust: In small bowl, combine crumbs, ground pecans and butter; mix well. Remove 1 cup (250 mL) crumb mixture and set aside. Press remaining crumbs evenly onto bottom of 9 ½-inch (24 cm) springform pan. Bake at 325 F (160 C) for 6 minutes or until set. Cool crust in pan on rack. *(Make ahead: Cooled crust can be covered with plastic wrap and stored at room temperature for up to 1 day.)*

Filling: In medium-size heavy saucepan, combine pumpkin, sugar, salt, cinnamon, ginger and nutmeg; stir in water. Place over medium heat and cook until mixture is hot, stirring constantly; continue cooking and stirring for an additional 4 minutes. Remove from heat and stir in brandy; return to heat and stir for 1 minute. Remove from heat and let cool slightly. Cover tightly and refrigerate overnight or until chilled.

When pumpkin mixture is well chilled, remove ice cream from container and put in large bowl. Refrigerate for 20 to 30 minutes or until ice cream has softened slightly, stirring occasionally. Add cooled pumpkin mixture to ice cream; stir to mix well. Spread half the softened ice cream mixture over crumb crust. Sprinkle with reserved crumb mixture. Spread remaining ice cream mixture evenly over top. Freeze for 1 hour or until just firm. Wrap in foil and freeze overnight. *(Make ahead: Can be frozen for up to 1 week.)*

Sauce: In heavy saucepan, combine cream, brown and granulated sugars, and butter. Place over medium-low heat; cook for 4 minutes or until sugar dissolves, stirring constantly. Increase heat to medium; bring sauce to a simmer, stirring frequently. Cook for 12 minutes, stirring constantly. Remove from heat; stir in brandy. Let cool until just warm. *(Make ahead: Put cooled sauce in microwaveable bowl; cover tightly with plastic wrap and refrigerate for up to 3 days. To reheat, microwave, uncovered, on Medium for about 1 ½ minutes or until just warm, stirring twice.)* Stir in chopped pecans.

When ready to serve, remove side of pan and let ice cream torte stand at room temperature for 5 minutes. Cut into wedges and top with warm caramel sauce. Garnish with pecan halves and serve immediately.

Tips

• *We tried melting store-bought caramel candies hoping this would be a good substitute for home-made caramel sauce — don't be tempted, the home-made caramel sauce is far superior in flavour.*

• *Don't be intimidated by the length of this recipe. The crust, caramel sauce and cooking the pumpkin mixture can be done ahead of time. The assembled torte can be frozen for up to 1 week.*

Makes 12 servings. PER SERVING: 688 cal, 6 g pro, 37 g fat, 86 g carb.

Almond Roca Ice Cream Torte

1	(200 g) package chocolate wafers, broken into large pieces
½	cup (125 mL) butter, melted
8	cups (2 L) coffee-flavoured ice cream
¾	cup (175 mL) slivered almonds, toasted
1	tablespoon (15 mL) Kahlua
¾	cup (175 mL) chopped Almond Roca candy (4 ounces/125 g)
1	ounce (30 g) bittersweet chocolate, shaved

In food processor, pulse wafers until fine crumbs form (about 2½ cups/625 mL). In medium bowl, combine wafer crumbs and butter. Reserve 1 cup (250 mL) crumb mixture and press remaining onto bottom of 9-inch (23 cm) springform pan. Refrigerate while preparing filling.

Remove ice cream from container and put in large bowl. Refrigerate for 20 to 30 minutes or until softened slightly, stirring occasionally. Stir in almonds and Kahlua.

Spread half the softened ice cream mixture over crumb crust. Combine half the chopped candy with reserved crumb mixture and sprinkle evenly over ice cream in pan, pressing lightly. Spread remaining ice cream over top. Sprinkle outside edge of torte with shaved chocolate and remaining chopped candy. Wrap completely in foil and freeze overnight.
(Make ahead: Can be frozen for up to 3 days.)

Run knife between torte and pan side to loosen; remove side of pan. Let torte stand at room temperature for 5 minutes. Cut into wedges and serve immediately.

Tip: *What is Almond Roca? It's a log-shaped buttercrunch confection made from almonds, butter and chocolate. One (140 g) box will yield a little more than ¾ cup (175 mL) chopped candy.*

Makes 12 servings. PER SERVING: 459 cal, 8 g pro, 29 g fat, 45 g carb.

Index

About The Nutritional Analysis

- The approximate nutritional analysis for each recipe does not include variations or optional ingredients. Figures are rounded off.

- Abbreviations: cal = calories, pro = protein, carb = carbohydrate

- The analysis is based on the first ingredient listed where there is a choice.